# low fat

simple and delicious easy-to-make recipes

Susanna Tee

p

This is a Parragon Publishing Book
First published in 2002

Parragon Publishing
Queen Street House
4 Queen Street
Bath, BA1 1HE, UK

ISBN: 0-75258-896-6

Printed in China

Produced by the Bridgewater Book Company Ltd.

**Photographer** Ian Parsons

**Home Economist** Sara Hesketh

## NOTES FOR THE READER

- This book uses both imperial and metric measurements. Follow the same units of measurement throughout; do not mix imperial and metric.

- All spoon measurements are level: teaspoons are assumed to be 5 ml, and tablespoons are assumed to be 15 ml.

- Unless otherwise stated, milk is assumed to be whole milk, eggs and individual vegetables such as carrots are medium, and pepper is freshly ground black pepper.

- Recipes using raw eggs should be avoided by infants, the elderly, pregnant women, convalescents, and anyone suffering from an illness.

- The times given are an approximate guide only. Preparation times differ according to the techniques used by different people and the cooking times may also vary from those given. Optional ingredients, variations, or serving suggestions have not been included in the calculations.

# contents

# introduction

This book will convince you that a lowfat diet need never be dreary. These healthy dishes are bursting with flavor. All are easy to prepare and good to eat. There are no complicated cooking methods involved or expensive ingredients to buy.

The recipes use fat-free or fat-reduced cooking methods, and all you need to do is to select lowfat dairy products, lean meats, such as skinless chicken and turkey, and the leanest cuts of beef, lamb, and pork, and of course, plenty of vegetables.

Vegetable oil spray also reduces the amount of fat used, for example when stir-frying, and nonstick liner is useful for lining cookie sheets. The only special equipment you need is a heavy, nonstick skillet or a nonstick wok.

When serving bread or vegetables with these dishes, don't be tempted to reach for the butter dish: simply eat delicious fresh bread and add a generous sprinkling of chopped herbs to the vegetables. Instead of rich salad dressings, make your own with lowfat yogurt or cottage cheese, or use a fat-reduced mayonnaise. You will soon be feeling healthier without feeling deprived of your favorite dishes.

| guide to recipe key | |
|---|---|
| easy | Recipes are graded as follows: 1 pea = easy; 2 peas = very easy; 3 peas = extremely easy. |
| serves 4 | Recipes generally serve four people. Simply halve the ingredients to serve two, taking care not to mix imperial and metric measurements. |
| 10 minutes | Preparation time. Where chilling is involved, this time has been added on separately: eg, 15 minutes + 1 hour to chill. |
| 10 minutes | Cooking time. |

greek feta salad
page 16

marinated lamb kabobs
page 56

cheese & spinach lasagna
page 64

raspberry creams
page 92

# light lunches & suppers

These are recipes that are easy to make yet satisfying to eat at a midday break or as a light evening meal. They are ideal served simply with fresh crusty bread and then followed with fresh fruit for a lowfat, healthy lunch or supper. Most of them—for example, Sweet Red Bell Pepper & Tomato Soup, and Greek Feta Salad can also be served as an appetizer as they are light and refreshing. Choose from delicious temptations such as Chilled Smoked Mackerel with Horseradish Dressing, Shrimp & Mango Salad, and Vegetable Frittata.

# sweet red bell pepper & tomato soup

| | | ingredients | |
|---|---|---|---|
| | extremely easy | 1 tbsp olive oil<br>2 tbsp water<br>2 red bell peppers, deseeded<br>  and chopped finely<br>1 garlic clove, chopped finely<br>1 onion, chopped finely | 14 oz/400 g canned<br>  chopped tomatoes<br>5 cups vegetable bouillon<br>salt and pepper<br><br>fresh basil leaves, to garnish |
| | serves 4 | | |
| | 5 minutes | | |
| | 30–35 minutes | | |

NUTRITIONAL
INFORMATION

| | |
|---|---|
| calories | 89 |
| protein | 3 g |
| carbohydrate | 12 g |
| sugars | 10 g |
| fat | 4 g |
| saturates | 0.5 g |

Put the oil, water, bell peppers, garlic, and onion in a pan, heat gently, and cook for 5–10 minutes, or until the vegetables have softened. Cover the pan and simmer for a further 10 minutes.

Add the tomatoes, bouillon, salt, and pepper and simmer, uncovered, for 15 minutes.

Serve garnished with basil leaves.

# mixed bean soup

| | | ingredients | |
|---|---|---|---|
| extremely easy | | 1 garlic clove, crushed | salt and pepper |
| | | 1 onion, chopped finely | pinch of dried mixed herbs |
| serves 4 | | 1 celery stalk, sliced finely | 14 oz/400 g canned red kidney beans, |
| | | 1 carrot, diced finely | drained and rinsed |
| | | 1 leek, sliced finely | 14 oz/400 g black-eye peas, drained |
| 10 minutes | | 14 oz/400 g canned | and rinsed |
| | | chopped tomatoes | |
| | | 2½ cups vegetable bouillon | warm crusty bread, to serve |
| 35 minutes | | | |

NUTRITIONAL
INFORMATION

| | |
|---|---|
| calories | 238 |
| protein | 16 g |
| carbohydrate | 42 g |
| sugars | 11 g |
| fat | 2 g |
| saturates | neg |

Put all the ingredients, except the beans, into a large pan. Bring to a boil, then simmer for 30 minutes, stirring occasionally, until the vegetables are tender.

Add the beans and simmer for a further 4–5 minutes, or until hot.

Serve with warm crusty bread.

# chicken & vegetable soup

| | | ingredients | |
|---|---|---|---|
| | extremely easy | 1 onion, chopped finely | 5⅔ cups chicken bouillon |
| | | 1 garlic clove, chopped finely | salt and pepper |
| | serves 4 | 1¼ cups shredded white cabbage | 1¼ cups diced cooked chicken |
| | | 2 medium carrots, chopped finely | |
| | | 4 potatoes, diced | chopped fresh parsley, to garnish |
| | 10 minutes | 1 green bell pepper, deseeded and diced | warm crusty bread, to serve |
| | | 14 oz/400 g canned chopped tomatoes | |
| | 1 hour 10 minutes | | |

**NUTRITIONAL INFORMATION**

| | |
|---|---|
| calories | 240 |
| protein | 19 g |
| carbohydrate | 37 g |
| sugars | 10 g |
| fat | 3 g |
| saturates | 0.5 g |

Put all the ingredients, except the chicken and parsley, in a large pan and bring to a boil. Simmer for 1 hour, or until the vegetables are tender.

Add the chicken and simmer for a further 10 minutes, or until hot.

Garnish with parsley and serve with warm crusty bread.

# tuna & fresh vegetable salad

| | | ingredients | |
|---|---|---|---|
| extremely easy | | DRESSING | 8 oz/225 g zucchini, sliced thinly |
| | | 4 tbsp reduced-calorie mayonnaise | 3¼ cups thinly sliced |
| serves 4 | | 4 tbsp lowfat plain yogurt | white mushrooms |
| | | 2 tbsp white wine vinegar | 12 oz/350 g canned tuna in brine, |
| | | salt and pepper | drained and flaked |
| 10 minutes + 1 hour to marinate | | 12 cherry tomatoes, halved | chopped fresh parsley, to garnish |
| | | 1½ cups whole green beans, | |
| | | cut into 1 inch/2.5 cm pieces | salad greens, to serve |
| — | | | |

**NUTRITIONAL INFORMATION**

| | |
|---|---|
| calories | 187 |
| protein | 26 g |
| carbohydrate | 8 g |
| sugars | 7 g |
| fat | 6 g |
| saturates | 0.5 g |

To make the dressing, put the mayonnaise, yogurt, vinegar, salt, and pepper in a screw-topped jar and shake together until the ingredients are well blended.

Put the tomatoes, beans, zucchini, and mushrooms in a bowl. Pour over the dressing and marinate for about 1 hour.

To serve, arrange the salad greens on a serving dish. Add the vegetables and then the tuna, and garnish with chopped parsley.

# greek feta salad

| | | ingredients | |
|---|---|---|---|
| extremely easy | | DRESSING | 4 tomatoes, sliced |
| | | 3 tbsp extra virgin olive oil | ½ cucumber, peeled and sliced |
| | | 1 tbsp lemon juice | 1 small red onion, sliced thinly |
| serves 4 | | ½ tsp dried oregano | 4 oz/115 g feta cheese, cubed |
| | | salt and pepper | 8 black olives |
| 10 minutes | | | a few grape leaves, to serve |
| — | | | |

NUTRITIONAL
INFORMATION

| | |
|---|---|
| calories | 186 |
| protein | 6 g |
| carbohydrate | 7 g |
| sugars | 6 g |
| fat | 15 g |
| saturates | 5 g |

To make the dressing, put the oil, lemon juice, oregano, salt, and pepper in a screw-topped jar and shake together until blended.

Arrange the grape leaves on a serving dish and then the tomatoes, cucumber, and onion. Sprinkle the cheese and olives on top. Pour the dressing over the salad and serve.

# shrimp & mango salad

| | | **ingredients** | |
|---|---|---|---|
| | extremely easy | 2 mangoes<br>2 cups peeled, cooked shrimp | 4 whole cooked shrimp, to garnish |
| | serves 4 | DRESSING<br>juice from the mangoes | salad greens, to serve |
| | 10 minutes | 6 tbsp lowfat plain yogurt<br>2 tbsp reduced-calorie mayonnaise<br>1 tbsp lemon juice<br>salt and pepper | |
| | — | | |

NUTRITIONAL
INFORMATION

| | |
|---|---|
| calories | 146 |
| protein | 16 g |
| carbohydrate | 15 g |
| sugars | 14 g |
| fat | 3 g |
| saturates | 0.5 g |

Cutting close to the pit, cut a large slice from one side of each mango, then cut another slice from the opposite side. Without breaking the skin, cut the flesh in the segments into squares, then push the skin inside out to expose the cubes, and cut away from the skin. Use a sharp knife to peel the remaining center section and cut the flesh away from the pit into cubes. Reserve any juice in a bowl and put the mango flesh in a separate bowl.

Add the shrimp to the mango flesh. Add the yogurt, mayonnaise, lemon juice, salt, and pepper to the juice and blend together.

Arrange the salad greens on a serving dish and add the mango flesh and shrimp. Pour the dressing over them and serve garnished with the whole shrimp.

# warm chicken liver salad

| | | ingredients | |
|---|---|---|---|
| very easy | salad greens<br>1 tbsp olive oil<br>1 small onion, chopped finely<br>1 lb/450 g frozen chicken<br>  livers, thawed | 1 tsp chopped fresh tarragon<br>1 tsp wholegrain mustard<br>2 tbsp balsamic vinegar<br>salt and pepper | |
| serves 4 | | | |
| 5 minutes | | | |
| 10–12 minutes | | | |

**NUTRITIONAL INFORMATION**

| | |
|---|---|
| calories | 142 |
| protein | 21 g |
| carbohydrate | 2 g |
| sugars | 1 g |
| fat | 6 g |
| saturates | 1 g |

Arrange the salad greens on serving plates.

Heat the oil in a nonstick skillet, add the onion, and cook for 5 minutes, or until softened. Add the chicken livers, tarragon, and mustard and cook for 3–5 minutes, stirring, until tender. Put on top of the salad greens.

Add the vinegar, salt, and pepper to the skillet and heat, stirring constantly, until all the sediment has been lifted from the skillet. Pour the dressing over the chicken livers and serve warm.

# chilled smoked mackerel with horseradish dressing

| | | ingredients |
|---|---|---|
| | extremely easy | 4 smoked mackerel |
| | serves 4 | DRESSING<br>²⁄₃ cup lowfat<br>  plain yogurt |
| | 10 minutes + at least 30 minutes to chill | 1 tsp grated horseradish<br>salt and pepper |
| | — | watercress sprigs or mizuna, `<br>to garnish |

**NUTRITIONAL INFORMATION**

| | |
|---|---|
| calories | 376 |
| protein | 21 g |
| carbohydrate | 3 g |
| sugars | 3 g |
| fat | 31 g |
| saturates | 6 g |

Remove the skin from the mackerel fillets, then cut each fillet in half lengthwise. Chill in the refrigerator for at least 30 minutes.

Meanwhile, combine the yogurt, horseradish, salt, and pepper. Chill in the refrigerator with the mackerel.

To serve, arrange the mackerel on serving plates, spoon the horseradish dressing over it, and garnish with watercress sprigs or mizuna.

# vegetable frittata

| | | ingredients | |
|---|---|---|---|
| easy | 4 eggs<br>2 egg whites<br>salt and pepper<br>1 tsp olive oil<br>1 onion, chopped coarsely<br>1 garlic clove, chopped finely | 1 green bell pepper, deseeded and<br>  chopped finely<br>1 zucchini, sliced thickly<br>8 oz/225 g cooked potatoes, diced<br>1 tomato, chopped coarsely<br>½ cup grated reduced-fat mozzarella | |
| serves 4 | | | |
| 10 minutes | | | |
| 20–30 minutes | | | |

**NUTRITIONAL INFORMATION**

| | |
|---|---|
| calories | 215 |
| protein | 13 g |
| carbohydrate | 15 g |
| sugars | 5 g |
| fat | 12 g |
| saturates | 4 g |

Beat the whole eggs and egg whites in a bowl and season with salt and pepper.

Heat the oil in a large nonstick skillet and add the onion, garlic, and green bell pepper. Cook for 5 minutes, or until softened. Add the zucchini and potatoes and cook for a further 5–10 minutes, or until lightly browned. Stir in the tomato.

Pour in the egg mixture and cook over low heat for 5–10 minutes, or until the mixture is set and only the top is runny. Sprinkle the cheese over the top.

Transfer the pan to a preheated broiler and cook until the top is set, but not hard, and the cheese has melted and begun to brown. Serve hot, cut into wedges.

# homemade
# turkey burgers

| | | ingredients | |
|---|---|---|---|
| easy | | ¼ cup long grain white rice | 1 garlic clove, chopped finely |
| | | salt and pepper | 1 tsp ground sage |
| serves 8 | | 1 lb/450 g lean ground turkey | ½ tsp dried thyme |
| | | 1 small cooking apple, peeled, | ½ tsp ground allspice |
| | |   cored, and grated | vegetable oil spray, for frying |
| 15 minutes | | 1 small onion, chopped finely | |
| 20 minutes | | | |

**NUTRITIONAL
INFORMATION**

| | |
|---|---|
| calories | 161 |
| protein | 26 g |
| carbohydrate | 10 g |
| sugars | 5 g |
| fat | 2 g |
| saturates | 1 g |

Cook the rice in a large pan of boiling salted water for about 10 minutes, or until tender. Drain, rinse under cold running water, then drain well again.

Put the cooked rice and all the remaining ingredients in a large bowl and mix well together. With wet hands, shape the mixture into 8 thick burgers.

Spray a large, nonstick skillet with oil, add the burgers, and cook for about 10 minutes, turning them over several times, until they are golden brown. Remove from the skillet and serve while hot.

# main courses

The following recipes show just how easy it is to prepare lowfat dishes. They all use lean cuts of meat, poultry, and fish that are seasoned with fresh vegetables, herbs, and spices, and are packed with flavor. There are recipes for family meals and entertaining, and recipes for warm summer evenings or cold winter's nights. Choose from such dishes as Moussaka, Chicken with a Honey Glazed Crust, Marinated Lamb Kabobs, and Broiled Salmon with Red Bell Pepper Sauce. All are mouthwatering—the only difficulty is deciding which to choose!

# mexican chicken burritos

| | | ingredients | |
|---|---|---|---|
| very easy | | 8 wheat flour tortillas | 1 packet taco seasoning |
| | | vegetable oil spray | 4 tomatoes, chopped coarsely |
| serves 4 | | 1 onion, chopped finely | 4 scallions, sliced thinly |
| | | 4 skinless, boneless chicken breast | |
| | | portions, sliced thinly | 1 tub tomato salsa, to serve |
| 10 minutes | | | |
| 30 minutes | | | |

**NUTRITIONAL INFORMATION**

| | |
|---|---|
| calories | 473 |
| protein | 40 g |
| carbohydrate | 75 g |
| sugars | 7 g |
| fat | 4 g |
| saturates | 1 g |

Preheat the oven to 300°F/150°C.

Wrap the tortillas in aluminum foil and cook in the oven for 10 minutes, or until soft.

Meanwhile, spray a large nonstick skillet with oil. Add the onion and cook for 5 minutes, or until softened. Add the chicken. Stirring occasionally, cook for 5 minutes, or until tender. Stir in the taco seasoning.

Preheat the oven to 350°F/180°C. Put the chicken mixture in the center of each tortilla and add the tomatoes and scallions. Fold the tortillas into a packet and put in an ovenproof dish.

Cover the dish and cook in the preheated oven for 20 minutes. Spoon the tomato salsa over the hot tortillas before serving.

# chicken with
# a honey-glazed crust

| | | ingredients |
|---|---|---|
| very easy | | 3 tbsp wheat germ |
| | serves 4 | 3 tbsp honey |
| | | 1 tbsp French mustard |
| | | 4 skinless chicken breast portions |
| | 5 minutes | salad greens (optional), to serve |
| | 30–40 minutes | |

**NUTRITIONAL INFORMATION**

| | |
|---|---|
| calories | 194 |
| protein | 31 g |
| carbohydrate | 13 g |
| sugars | 12 g |
| fat | 2 g |
| saturates | 0.5 g |

Preheat the oven to 375°F/190°C.

Put the wheat germ, honey, and mustard in a bowl and mix well together. Put the chicken breast portions on a cookie sheet and spread with the honey mixture.

Bake the chicken in the oven for 30–40 minutes, or until the chicken is tender and a crust has formed. Remove from the oven and transfer to warm serving dishes.

Serve with salad greens, if you like.

# italian braised
# chicken & fennel

| | | ingredients |
|---|---|---|
| | very easy | 4 tomatoes, chopped finely |
| | | 1 garlic clove, crushed |
| | | ¼ cup white wine |
| | serves 4 | 2 tsp balsamic vinegar |
| | | salt and pepper |
| | | 4 skinless chicken breast portions |
| | 5 minutes | 4 small fennel bulbs, quartered |
| | | |
| | | flat leaf parsley, to garnish |
| | 35 minutes | |

**NUTRITIONAL INFORMATION**

| | |
|---|---|
| calories | 166 |
| protein | 32 g |
| carbohydrate | 5 g |
| sugars | 5 g |
| fat | 2 g |
| saturates | 0.5 g |

Put the tomatoes, garlic, wine, vinegar, salt, and pepper in a large, nonstick skillet and bring to a boil. Reduce the heat and add the chicken and fennel pieces. Cover and simmer for about 30 minutes, or until the chicken and fennel are tender.

Using a slotted spoon, transfer the chicken and fennel to warm serving plates.

Bring the sauce to a boil and cook, stirring occasionally, until thickened slightly. Spoon the sauce over the chicken and serve garnished with parsley.

# tandoori chicken

| | | ingredients | |
|---|---|---|---|
| ◿ | very easy | 4–8 skinless chicken portions | 1 tsp garam masala |
| | | | ½ tsp salt |
| ◢ | serves 4 | MARINADE | ½ tsp cayenne pepper, optional |
| | | 1 small onion, quartered | 2 tbsp lemon or lime juice |
| | | 2 garlic cloves | 4 tbsp lowfat plain yogurt |
| ◓ | 10 minutes + 24 hours to marinate | 1 tsp chopped fresh ginger | ¼ tsp red food coloring |
| | | 2 tsp ground cumin | |
| | | 2 tsp ground coriander | lemon or lime wedges, to garnish |
| ◷ | 45 minutes to 1 hour | | |

NUTRITIONAL
INFORMATION

| | |
|---|---|
| calories | 160 |
| protein | 50 g |
| carbohydrate | 4 g |
| sugars | 3 g |
| fat | 20 g |
| saturates | 1 g |

Using a sharp knife, cut ½ inch/1 cm deep slashes in each piece of chicken and put in a shallow dish.

Put all the remaining ingredients in a food processor and process until smooth. Spread the marinade over the chicken pieces, working it into the cuts in the flesh. Cover the dish and marinate in the refrigerator for 24 hours.

Preheat the oven to 400°F/200°C.

Place the chicken pieces on a rack in a roasting pan and cook in the oven for 45 minutes to 1 hour, turning the pieces over once and basting with the juices in the pan, until tender.

Serve garnished with lemon or lime wedges.

# herb-crusted haddock
# with tomato salsa

| | | ingredients | |
|---|---|---|---|
| | very easy | 2 cups fresh white bread crumbs | vegetable oil spray |
| | | 3 tbsp lemon juice | 4 haddock fillets |
| | serves 4 | 1 tbsp pesto sauce | |
| | | 2 tbsp chopped fresh parsley | 1 tub tomato salsa, to serve |
| | | salt and pepper | |
| | 10 minutes | | |
| | 10–15 minutes | | |

**NUTRITIONAL INFORMATION**

| | |
|---|---|
| calories | 245 |
| protein | 41 g |
| carbohydrate | 16 g |
| sugars | 2 g |
| fat | 2 g |
| saturates | 0 g |

Put the bread crumbs, 2 tablespoons of the lemon juice, the pesto sauce, parsley, salt, and pepper in a bowl and mix well together.

Line a broiler pan with aluminum foil and spray with vegetable oil. Place the haddock fillets on the foil and sprinkle with the remaining tablespoon of lemon juice and more salt and pepper. Cook under a preheated broiler for 5 minutes.

Turn the haddock fillets over and spread the herb and bread crumb mixture over the top of each.

Cook for a further 5–10 minutes, or until the haddock is tender and the crust is golden brown.

Serve with the tomato salsa spooned over the top of each fish.

# broiled salmon with
# red bell pepper sauce

| | | ingredients | |
|---|---|---|---|
| easy | | 3 red bell peppers | 1 onion, chopped finely |
| | | vegetable oil spray | 1 garlic clove, chopped finely |
| serves 4 | | 4 salmon steaks | 2 tsp balsamic vinegar |
| | | 1 tbsp lemon juice | handful of fresh basil leaves |
| | | salt and pepper | |
| 15 minutes | | | |
| 35–45 minutes | | | |

**NUTRITIONAL INFORMATION**

| | |
|---|---|
| calories | 326 |
| protein | 32 g |
| carbohydrate | 11 g |
| sugars | 10 g |
| fat | 17 g |
| saturates | 3 g |

Preheat the oven to 400°F/200°C.

Put the bell peppers on a cookie sheet and roast in the oven for 25 minutes, turning once, until deflated and slightly charred. Let cool, then peel off the skins and discard with the core and seeds.

Meanwhile, line a broiler pan with aluminum foil and spray with oil. Place the salmon steaks on the foil, sprinkle with lemon juice, salt, and pepper, and cook under a preheated broiler for 10–20 minutes, turning once, until tender.

Spray a small nonstick pan with oil and fry the onion and garlic for 5 minutes, or until softened. Process in a food processor with the bell pepper flesh, vinegar, basil, salt, and pepper until smooth. Return the mixture to the pan and reheat gently.

Serve the red bell pepper sauce with the cooked salmon steaks.

# baked fish & fries

| | | ingredients |
|---|---|---|
| | very easy | 450 g/1 lb mealy potatoes, peeled and |
| | | cut into thick, even French fries |
| | serves 4 | vegetable oil spray |
| | | ½ cup all-purpose white flour |
| | | 1 egg |
| | 20 minutes | 1 cup fresh white bread crumbs, |
| | | seasoned with salt and pepper |
| | | 4 cod or haddock fillets |
| | 40–45 minutes | |

**NUTRITIONAL INFORMATION**

| | |
|---|---|
| calories | 322 |
| protein | 37 g |
| carbohydrate | 37 g |
| sugars | 1 g |
| fat | 4 g |
| saturates | 1 g |

Preheat the oven to 400°F/200°C. Line 2 cookie sheets with nonstick liner.

Rinse the sliced potatoes under cold running water, then dry well on a clean dish towel. Put in a bowl, spray with oil, and toss together until coated. Spread the fries on a cookie sheet and cook in the oven for 40–45 minutes, turning once, until golden.

Meanwhile, put the flour on a plate, beat the egg in a shallow dish, and spread the seasoned bread crumbs on a large plate. Dip the fish fillets in the flour to coat, then the egg, letting any excess drip off, and finally the bread crumbs, patting them firmly into the fish. Place the fish in a single layer on a cookie sheet.

Fifteen minutes before the fries have cooked, bake the fish fillets in the oven for 10–15 minutes, turning them once during cooking, until the fish is tender. Serve the fish with the fries.

# red snapper
# with citrus fruit

| | | ingredients | |
|---|---|---|---|
| | very easy | MARINADE<br>6 tbsp fresh orange juice<br>3 tbsp lemon juice<br>3 tbsp lime juice<br>4 tbsp dry sherry<br>1 tsp chopped garlic<br>1 tsp chopped fresh ginger<br>salt and pepper | vegetable oil spray, for frying<br>4 red snapper<br><br>orange segments, to garnish |
| | serves 4 | | |
| | 10 minutes<br>+ 4 hours<br>to marinate | | |
| | 10–15<br>minutes | | |

NUTRITIONAL
INFORMATION

| | |
|---|---|
| calories | 194 |
| protein | 28 g |
| carbohydrate | 3 g |
| sugars | 3 g |
| fat | 6 g |
| saturates | 0 g |

Put all the marinade ingredients in a shallow dish and mix them well together.

Using a sharp knife, slash the snapper 3 times on each side. Add the fish to the marinade and marinate in the refrigerator, turning once or twice, for about 4 hours.

Line a broiler pan with aluminum foil and spray with vegetable oil. Place the fish on the foil and cook under a preheated broiler for 10–15 minutes, turning once and spooning over the marinade, until the flesh is tender.

Serve garnished with orange segments.

# flounder packets
# with fresh herbs

| | | ingredients | |
|---|---|---|---|
| | very easy | vegetable oil spray<br>4 flounder fillets, skinned<br>6 tbsp chopped fresh herbs,<br>　such as dill, parsley, chives,<br>　thyme, or marjoram | finely grated rind and juice<br>　of 2 lemons<br>1 small onion, sliced thinly<br>1 tbsp capers, rinsed (optional)<br>salt and pepper |
| | serves 4 | | |
| | 10 minutes | | |
| | 15 minutes | | |

NUTRITIONAL
INFORMATION

| | |
|---|---|
| calories | 129 |
| protein | 25 g |
| carbohydrate | 2 g |
| sugars | 1 g |
| fat | 2 g |
| saturates | 0 g |

Preheat the oven to 375°F/190°C. Cut 4 large squares of aluminum foil, each large enough to hold a fish and form a packet, and spray with oil.

Place each fish fillet on a foil sheet and sprinkle them with the herbs, lemon rind and juice, onion, capers (if using), salt. and pepper. Fold the foil to make a secure packet and place on a cookie sheet.

Bake the packets in the oven for 15 minutes, or until tender.

Serve the fish piping hot, in their loosely opened packets.

# stir-fried beef & snow peas

| | | ingredients | |
|---|---|---|---|
| | very easy | 1 lb/450 g round or sirloin steak, sliced thinly | 1 carrot, sliced thinly |
| | serves 4 | 2 tbsp soy sauce | 1 lb/450 g snow peas |
| | | 5 tbsp hoisin sauce | 8 oz/225 g canned sliced bamboo shoots, drained |
| | | 2 tbsp dry sherry | |
| | 10 minutes | vegetable oil spray | fresh sprigs of cilantro, to garnish |
| | | 1 onion, sliced thinly | |
| | | 1 tsp chopped fresh garlic | cooked rice or noodles, to serve |
| | 10 minutes | 1 tsp chopped fresh ginger | |

NUTRITIONAL
INFORMATION

| | |
|---|---|
| calories | 249 |
| protein | 33 g |
| carbohydrate | 15 g |
| sugars | 12 g |
| fat | 6 g |
| saturates | 2 g |

Put the strips of beef in a bowl, add the soy sauce, hoisin sauce, and sherry and stir together. Let marinate while you are cooking the vegetables.

Spray a large nonstick wok with oil. Add the onion, garlic, ginger, carrot, and snow peas and stir-fry for 5 minutes, or until softened.

Add the beef and marinade to the wok and stir-fry for 2–3 minutes, or until tender. Add the bamboo shoots and stir-fry for a further minute, until hot.

Transfer to a warm serving dish, garnish with cilantro, and serve with cooked rice or noodles, if you like.

# bœuf stroganoff

| | | ingredients | |
|---|---|---|---|
| very easy | | vegetable oil spray<br>1 onion, sliced coarsely<br>3¼ cups thinly sliced<br>  white mushrooms<br>1 tsp French mustard<br>1 lb/450 g round or sirloin steak,<br>  sliced thinly | 1¼ cups reduced-fat<br>  crème fraîche<br>salt and pepper<br><br>chopped fresh parsley, to garnish |
| serves 4 | | | |
| 5 minutes | | | |
| 15 minutes | | | |

**NUTRITIONAL INFORMATION**

| | |
|---|---|
| calories | 302 |
| protein | 30 g |
| carbohydrate | 7 g |
| sugars | 5 g |
| fat | 17 g |
| saturates | 11 g |

Spray a large, nonstick skillet with oil. Add the onion and cook, stirring, for 5 minutes, until softened and lightly colored.

Add the mushrooms and mustard to the skillet and cook, stirring occasionally, for a further 4–5 minutes, or until lightly colored.

Add the beef to the skillet and cook, stirring occasionally, for 5 minutes, or until tender. Add the crème fraîche and salt and pepper, then heat, stirring constantly, until hot.

Serve garnished with chopped parsley.

# linguine with shrimp

| | | **ingredients** | |
|---|---|---|---|
| | very easy | 12 oz/350 g linguine | 1 tsp chopped fresh garlic |
| | | salt and pepper | 1 tsp chopped fresh ginger |
| | serves 4 | 1 tbsp white wine vinegar | 2 cups peeled cooked shrimp |
| | | 1 tbsp lemon juice | 4 scallions, sliced thinly |
| | | 2 tbsp tomato paste | |
| | | pinch of sugar | chopped fresh parsley, to garnish |
| | 5 minutes | 6 tbsp water | |
| | 15 minutes | | |

**NUTRITIONAL INFORMATION**

| | |
|---|---|
| calories | 359 |
| protein | 21 g |
| carbohydrate | 68 g |
| sugars | 5 g |
| fat | 2 g |
| saturates | 0 g |

Cook the pasta in a large pan of boiling salted water for 10 minutes, or as directed on the packet, until tender.

Meanwhile, put the vinegar, lemon juice, tomato paste, sugar, water, salt, and pepper in a bowl and mix together.

Put the garlic, ginger, shrimp, and scallions in a large, heavy nonstick skillet and heat gently for 1–2 minutes, stirring constantly, until hot.

Drain the cooked pasta and add to the skillet. Combine with the sauce mixture and heat, stirring, until the pasta is well coated and the sauce is heated through.

Serve garnished with chopped parsley.

# moussaka

| | | ingredients | |
|---|---|---|---|
| | easy | 2 eggplants, sliced thinly | salt and pepper |
| | | 1 lb/450 g lean ground beef | 2 eggs |
| | serves 4 | 2 onions, sliced thinly | 1¼ cups lowfat |
| | | 1 tsp finely chopped garlic | plain yogurt |
| | | 14 oz/400 g canned tomatoes | 1 tbsp grated Parmesan cheese |
| | 40 minutes | 2 tbsp chopped fresh parsley | |
| | 45 minutes | | |

**NUTRITIONAL INFORMATION**

| | |
|---|---|
| calories | 357 |
| protein | 36 g |
| carbohydrate | 17 g |
| sugars | 15 g |
| fat | 16 g |
| saturates | 7 g |

In a large nonstick skillet, dry-fry the eggplant slices, in batches, on both sides until brown. Remove from the skillet.

Add the beef to the pan and cook for 5 minutes, stirring, until browned. Stir in the onions and garlic and cook for 5 minutes, or until lightly browned. Add the tomatoes, parsley, salt, and pepper, then bring the mixture to a boil, and simmer for 20 minutes, or until the meat is tender.

Preheat the oven to 350°F/180°C. Arrange half the eggplant slices in a layer in an ovenproof dish. Add the meat mixture, then a final layer of the remaining eggplant slices.

In a bowl, beat the eggs, then beat in the yogurt, and add salt and pepper. Pour the mixture over the eggplants and sprinkle the grated cheese on top. Bake the moussaka in the oven for 45 minutes, or until golden brown. Serve straight from the dish.

# marinated lamb kabobs

|  | |
|---|---|
| very easy | |
| serves 4 | |
| 10 minutes + 2–3 hours to marinate | |
| 15–20 minutes | |

### ingredients

MARINADE
⅔ cup lowfat
  plain yogurt
4 tbsp chopped fresh cilantro
2 tsp chopped garlic
2 tsp chopped fresh ginger
1 tsp ground coriander
1 tsp ground cumin
salt and pepper

1 lb/450 g leg of lamb, cut into
  1 inch/2.5 cm cubes

chopped fresh parsley, to garnish

salad, to serve

NUTRITIONAL
INFORMATION

| calories | 200 |
|---|---|
| protein | 25 g |
| carbohydrate | 3 g |
| sugars | 3 g |
| fat | 10 g |
| saturates | 4 g |

Put all the marinade ingredients into a large bowl and mix together. Stir in the lamb until coated in the marinade, then marinate in the refrigerator for 2–3 hours.

Thread the lamb cubes onto metal or bamboo skewers. Cook under a preheated broiler for 15–20 minutes, turning frequently and basting with the marinade, until tender.

Garnish with chopped parsley and serve with salad.

# quick-fried pork
# & pears

| | | ingredients | |
|---|---|---|---|
| | very easy | 1 tbsp soy sauce | 2 large pears |
| | | 1 tsp white wine vinegar | 4 scallions, sliced thinly |
| | serves 4 | 2 tbsp dry sherry | 1 tsp chopped garlic |
| | | 1 lb/450 g pork tenderloin, sliced very thinly | 1 tbsp chopped fresh ginger |
| | 15 minutes | | |
| | 5–7 minutes | | |

NUTRITIONAL
INFORMATION

| | |
|---|---|
| calories | 210 |
| protein | 25 g |
| carbohydrate | 9 g |
| sugars | 8 g |
| fat | 7 g |
| saturates | 2 g |

Put the soy sauce, vinegar, and sherry in a large bowl. Add the pork and mix together. Cut the pears into ¼ inch/5 mm slices, discarding the cores.

Reserve the green part of the scallions to use as garnish. Put the garlic, ginger, and scallions in a large nonstick wok and heat for 1–2 minutes, stirring constantly, until hot.

Add the pork mixture to the wok and stir-fry for 3–4 minutes, or until tender and beginning to brown. Add the pears and stir-fry for a further minute, or until hot.

Serve the stir-fry immediately, sprinkled with the sliced green scallion stems.

# vegetarian dishes

Vegetables are the perfect lowfat food and in this section is a collection of recipes using just vegetables as a main course. They illustrate how interesting and varied vegetables can be, but fortunately you don't have to be a vegetarian to enjoy them! You will find lowfat recipes for Cheese & Spinach Lasagna, Vegetable Biryani, Glazed Vegetable Kabobs, and Stuffed Eggplants, among other delicious dishes. Their flavor and freshness have been brought out to the full to provide nutritious and satisfying meals.

# spring vegetable risotto

| | | **ingredients** | |
|---|---|---|---|
| | easy | 3¾ cups vegetable bouillon | ¾ cup whole green beans, |
| | | 2 tsp olive oil | cut into 1 inch/2.5 cm pieces |
| | serves 4 | 1 small leek, sliced thinly | 3 cups risotto rice |
| | | 1 tsp chopped garlic | ⅔ cup dry white wine |
| | | 1 carrot, sliced thinly | ½ cup frozen baby |
| | | 2 zucchini, sliced thinly | peas, thawed |
| | 15 minutes | ¾ cup snow peas | salt and pepper |
| | 30–35 minutes | | |

**NUTRITIONAL INFORMATION**

| | |
|---|---|
| calories | 429 |
| protein | 10 g |
| carbohydrate | 36 g |
| sugars | 14 g |
| fat | 16 g |
| saturates | 9 g |

Pour the bouillon into a pan, bring to a boil, then keep at barely simmering point.

Meanwhile, heat the oil in a large, nonstick pan, add the leek, garlic, carrot, zucchini, snow peas, and beans and cook, stirring frequently, for 5 minutes, or until beginning to soften but not brown.

Add the rice and stir well for 2–3 minutes, or until coated in the oil. Add the wine and cook, stirring, until almost evaporated.

Add about ⅔ cup of the bouillon and cook gently, stirring occasionally, until absorbed. Add more bouillon, in ⅔ cup measures, as soon as each measure has been absorbed, stirring frequently. Continue until the rice is thick, creamy and tender. This will take 20–25 minutes. Stir in the peas, season with salt and pepper, and serve.

# cheese & spinach lasagna

| | | **ingredients** |
|---|---|---|
| very easy | | 1 lb/450 g frozen spinach, thawed     8 oz/225 g reduced fat mozzarella |
| | serves 4 | salt and pepper        cheese, sliced thinly |
| | | 2 cups lowfat ricotta cheese     1 tbsp freshly grated Parmesan cheese |
| | | 8 sheets no-precook lasagna |
| | 15 minutes | 2¼ cups strained bottled tomatoes     salad (optional), to serve |
| | 45–50 minutes | |

**NUTRITIONAL INFORMATION**

| | |
|---|---|
| calories | 369 |
| protein | 23 g |
| carbohydrate | 36 g |
| sugars | 14 g |
| fat | 16 g |
| saturates | 9 g |

Preheat the oven to 350°F/180°C.

Put the spinach in a strainer and squeeze out as much excess liquid as possible. Put half in the bottom of an ovenproof dish and add salt and pepper.

Spread half the ricotta over the spinach, cover with half the lasagna sheets, then spoon over half the strained bottled tomatoes. Arrange half the mozzarella slices on top. Repeat the layers and finally sprinkle over the Parmesan cheese.

Bake in the oven for 45–50 minutes, by which time the top should be brown and bubbling.

Serve with salad, if you like.

# pasta with ricotta
# & sun-dried tomatoes

| | | **ingredients** | |
|---|---|---|---|
| very easy | | 12 oz/350 g dried tagliatelle | GARNISH |
| | | salt and pepper | freshly grated Parmesan cheese |
| serves 4 | | 2 cups sun-dried tomatoes | fresh basil leaves |
| | | in oil, drained | |
| | | 1¾ cups lowfat ricotta cheese | |
| 10 minutes | | 1 garlic clove, crushed | |
| 10 minutes | | | |

**NUTRITIONAL INFORMATION**

| | |
|---|---|
| calories | 542 |
| protein | 18 g |
| carbohydrate | 74 g |
| sugars | 8 g |
| fat | 22 g |
| saturates | 6 g |

Cook the pasta in a large pan of boiling salted water for 10 minutes or as directed on the packet, until tender.

Meanwhile, using scissors, cut the tomatoes into small pieces into a pan. Add the ricotta, garlic, salt, and pepper and heat very gently, without boiling.

Drain the pasta, add to the tomato mixture, and toss together.

Serve garnished with basil leaves and generously sprinkled with freshly grated Parmesan.

# penne primavera

<table>
<tr><td rowspan="2">very easy</td><td colspan="2">ingredients</td></tr>
<tr><td>1 cup baby corn<br>½ cup whole baby carrots</td><td>1 ¼ cups lowfat<br>plain yogurt</td></tr>
<tr><td rowspan="2">serves 4</td><td>salt and pepper<br>1 ¼ cups shelled fava beans<br>generous 1 cup whole green beans,</td><td>1 tbsp chopped fresh parsley<br>1 tbsp chopped fresh chives</td></tr>
<tr><td>   cut into 1 inch/2.5 cm pieces<br>3 cups dried penne</td><td>a few fresh chives, to garnish</td></tr>
<tr><td>10 minutes</td><td></td><td></td></tr>
<tr><td>20 minutes</td><td></td><td></td></tr>
</table>

NUTRITIONAL
INFORMATION

| | |
|---|---|
| calories | 398 |
| protein | 19 g |
| carbohydrate | 79 g |
| sugars | 11 g |
| fat | 3 g |
| saturates | 1 g |

Cook the corn and carrots in boiling salted water for 5 minutes, or until tender, then drain, and rinse under cold running water. Cook the fava beans and green beans in boiling salted water for 3–4 minutes, or until tender, then drain, and rinse under cold running water. If you like, slip the skins off the fava beans.

Cook the pasta in a large pan of boiling salted water for 10 minutes or as directed on the packet, until tender.

Meanwhile, put the yogurt, parsley, chopped chives, salt, and pepper in a bowl and mix together.

Drain the cooked pasta and return to the pan. Add the vegetables and yogurt sauce, heat gently, and toss together, until hot.

Serve garnished with a few lengths of chives.

# vegetable biryani

| | | **ingredients** | |
|---|---|---|---|
| | very easy | 1 onion, quartered | 1½ cups whole green beans, |
| | | 2 garlic cloves | cut into 1 inch/2.5 cm lengths |
| | serves 4 | 1 tsp chopped fresh ginger | ½ cauliflower head, cut into flowerets |
| | | 1 tsp ground coriander | 1¾ cups basmati rice |
| | | 1 tsp ground cumin | 2 whole cloves |
| | 10 minutes | 1 tsp ground turmeric | ¼ tsp cardamom seeds |
| | | ½ tsp chilli powder | 2 tbsp lime juice |
| | | salt and pepper | |
| | | 6¼ cups water | chopped fresh cilantro, to garnish |
| | 30 minutes | 2 carrots, sliced thickly | |

**NUTRITIONAL**
**INFORMATION**

| | |
|---|---|
| calories | 378 |
| protein | 11 g |
| carbohydrate | 80 g |
| sugars | 8 g |
| fat | 2 g |
| saturates | 0 g |

Put the onion, garlic, ginger, coriander, cumin, turmeric, chilli, salt, and pepper in a food processor and process until smooth.

Spoon the spice mixture into a large, nonstick pan and cook, stirring, for 2 minutes. Stir in 3¾ cups of the water and bring to a boil. Add the carrots, beans, and cauliflower and simmer for 15 minutes, or until tender.

Meanwhile, put the rice in a strainer and rinse under cold running water. Put in a pan with the remaining 2½ cups of water, the cloves, cardamom seeds, and salt. Bring to a boil, then simmer for 10 minutes, or until just tender.

Drain the rice and stir into the vegetables with the lime juice. Simmer gently until the rice is tender and the liquid has been absorbed. Serve garnished with cilantro.

# bean & vegetable chili

| | | **ingredients** | |
|---|---|---|---|
| | very easy | 4 tbsp vegetable bouillon | 14 oz/400 g canned chopped |
| | | 1 onion, chopped coarsely | tomatoes |
| | serves 4 | 1 green bell pepper, deseeded | salt and pepper |
| | | and chopped finely | 14 oz/400 g canned kidney |
| | | 1 red bell pepper, deseeded | beans, drained |
| | | and chopped finely | 14 oz/400 g canned black-eye |
| | 10 minutes | 1 tsp finely chopped garlic | peas, drained |
| | | 1 tsp finely chopped fresh ginger | |
| | | 2 tsp ground cumin | chopped fresh cilantro, to garnish |
| | 20 minutes | ½ tsp chili powder | |
| | | 2 tbsp tomato paste | fresh crusty bread, to serve |

NUTRITIONAL
INFORMATION

| | |
|---|---|
| calories | 246 |
| protein | 17 g |
| carbohydrate | 44 g |
| sugars | 14 g |
| fat | 2 g |
| saturates | 0 g |

Heat the bouillon in a large pan, add the onion and bell peppers and simmer for 5 minutes, or until softened.

Stir in the garlic, ginger, cumin, chili powder, tomato paste, tomatoes (together with their juice), salt, and pepper and simmer for 10 minutes. Stir in the kidney beans and black-eye peas and simmer for a further 5 minutes, or until hot. Remove the pan from the heat and transfer the chili to a warm serving dish.

Garnish with chopped cilantro and serve with fresh crusty bread.

# glazed vegetable kabobs

|  |  | **ingredients** | |
|---|---|---|---|
| | very easy | ²/₃ cup lowfat <br> plain yogurt <br> 4 tbsp mango chutney <br> 1 tsp chopped garlic <br> 1 tbsp lemon juice <br> salt and pepper <br> 8 baby onions, peeled | 16 baby corn, halved <br> 2 zucchini, cut into <br> 1 inch/2.5 cm pieces <br> 16 white mushrooms <br> 16 cherry tomatoes <br><br> salad greens, to garnish |
| | serves 4 | | |
| | 15 minutes | | |
| | 10 minutes | | |

**NUTRITIONAL INFORMATION**

| | |
|---|---|
| calories | 144 |
| protein | 8 g |
| carbohydrate | 26 g |
| sugars | 24 g |
| fat | 1 g |
| saturates | 0 g |

Put the yogurt, chutney, garlic, lemon juice, salt, and pepper in a bowl and stir together.

Put the onions in a pan of boiling water. Return to a boil, then drain well.

Thread the onions, corn, zucchini, mushrooms, and tomatoes alternately onto 8 metal or bamboo skewers.

Arrange the kabobs on a broiler pan and brush with the yogurt glaze. Cook under a preheated broiler for 10 minutes, turning and brushing frequently, until golden and tender.

Serve with a garnish of mixed salad greens.

# stuffed eggplants

| | | ingredients | |
|---|---|---|---|
| easy | | 2 eggplants<br>1 onion, chopped finely<br>1 tsp chopped garlic<br>1½ cups coarsely chopped<br>  white mushrooms | 2 tsp chopped fresh cilantro<br>1 cup fresh bread crumbs<br>salt and pepper<br>2 oz/55 g feta cheese,<br>  crumbled finely |
| serves 4 | | | |
| 15 minutes | | | |
| 45 minutes | | | |

**NUTRITIONAL INFORMATION**

| | |
|---|---|
| calories | 104 |
| protein | 5 g |
| carbohydrate | 13 g |
| sugars | 5 g |
| fat | 4 g |
| saturates | 2 g |

Put the eggplants in a large pan of boiling water and cook for 20 minutes, or until tender. Drain well.

Cut the eggplants in half lengthwise, scoop out the flesh, and chop finely. Reserve the eggplant shells.

Preheat the oven to 350°F/180°C.

Put the eggplant flesh, onion, garlic, mushrooms, and cilantro in a nonstick skillet and cook for 5 minutes. Stir in the bread crumbs, salt, and pepper.

Stuff the eggplant shells with the mixture and sprinkle with the feta cheese.

Place on a cookie sheet and bake in the oven for 20 minutes. Transfer to warm serving plates and serve immediately.

# puddings & desserts

The lowfat pudding and dessert recipes in
this chapter use fresh or dried fruits and
are bursting with tempting flavors.
There is a selection of both hot puddings
and cold desserts, such as Apple Strudel
with Warm Cider Sauce, Apricot and
Orange Fool, and Raspberry Creams.
Don't forget that old favorite, Fresh Fruit
Salad. Simply use fruits in season and dress
them with your choice of fresh fruit juice.
You will find that all these recipes will
bring an enjoyable finale to any meal.

# golden baked
# apple pudding

| | | **ingredients** |
|---|---|---|
| | very easy | 1 lb/450 g cooking apples |
| | | 1 tsp ground cinnamon |
| | serves 4 | 2 tbsp golden raisins |
| | | 4 oz/115 g whole-wheat bread, about 4 thick slices |
| | 15 minutes | generous ½ cup lowfat cottage cheese |
| | | 4 tbsp light brown sugar |
| | 30–35 minutes | generous 1 cup lowfat milk |

**NUTRITIONAL INFORMATION**

| | |
|---|---|
| calories | 227 |
| protein | 5 g |
| carbohydrate | 52 g |
| sugars | 40 g |
| fat | 2 g |
| saturates | 1 g |

Preheat the oven to 425°F/220°C.

Peel and core the apples and chop the flesh into ½ inch/1 cm pieces. Put the apple pieces in a bowl and toss with the cinnamon and golden raisins.

Remove the crusts and cut the bread into ½ inch/1 cm cubes. Add to the apples with the cottage cheese and 3 tablespoons of the brown sugar, and mix together. Stir in the milk.

Turn the mixture into an ovenproof dish and sprinkle with the remaining sugar. Bake in the oven for 30–35 minutes, or until golden brown. Serve hot.

# apricot & orange fool

| | | **ingredients** |
|---|---|---|
| extremely easy | | generous 1 cup ready-to-eat |
| | | dried apricots |
| serves 4 | | 1 tbsp honey |
| | | generous 1 cup fresh orange juice |
| | | generous 1 cup lowfat |
| 5 minutes | | plain yogurt |
| | | 2 tsp flaked almonds (toasted), |
| | | to decorate |
| — | | |

**NUTRITIONAL INFORMATION**

| | |
|---|---|
| calories | 171 |
| protein | 6 g |
| carbohydrate | 37 g |
| sugars | 37 g |
| fat | 1 g |
| saturates | 0 g |

Put all the ingredients, except the almonds, in a food processor and process until smooth.

Serve in individual glass dishes, decorated with toasted almonds.

# spiced baked pears

| | | ingredients |
|---|---|---|
| | extremely easy | 4 large, firm eating pears<br>$\frac{2}{3}$ cup apple juice<br>1 cinnamon stick<br>4 whole cloves<br>1 bay leaf |
| | serves 4 | |
| | 5 minutes | |
| | 30 minutes | |

**NUTRITIONAL INFORMATION**

| | |
|---|---|
| calories | 114 |
| protein | 1 g |
| carbohydrate | 29 g |
| sugars | 29 g |
| fat | 0 g |
| saturates | 0 g |

Preheat the oven to 350°F/180°C.

Peel and core the pears and cut them into quarters. Place in an ovenproof dish and add the remaining ingredients.

Cover the dish and bake in the oven for 30 minutes.

Serve the pears hot or cold.

# apple strudel with warm cider sauce

| | | ingredients | |
|---|---|---|---|
| easy | | 8 crisp eating apples | SAUCE |
| | | 1 tbsp lemon juice | 1 tbsp cornstarch |
| serves 2–4 | | ⅔ cup golden raisins | 2 cups hard cider |
| | | 1 tsp ground cinnamon | |
| | | ½ tsp grated nutmeg | confectioners' sugar, to serve |
| 25 minutes | | 1 tbsp light brown sugar | |
| | | 6 sheets phyllo pastry | |
| | | vegetable oil spray | |
| 15–20 minutes | | | |

NUTRITIONAL
INFORMATION

| | |
|---|---|
| calories | 283 |
| protein | 3 g |
| carbohydrate | 61 g |
| sugars | 47 g |
| fat | 1 g |
| saturates | 0 g |

Preheat the oven to 375°F/190°C. Line a cookie sheet with nonstick liner.

Peel and core the apples and chop them into ½ inch/1 cm dice. Toss the pieces in a bowl, with the lemon juice, golden raisins, cinnamon, nutmeg, and sugar.

Lay out a sheet of phyllo, spray with vegetable oil, and lay a second sheet on top. Repeat with a third sheet. Spread over half the apple mixture and roll up lengthwise, tucking in the ends to enclose the filling. Repeat to make a second strudel. Slide onto the cookie sheet, spray with oil, and bake for 15–20 minutes.

Blend the cornstarch in a pan with a little hard cider until smooth. Add the remaining cider and heat gently, stirring, until the mixture boils and thickens. Serve the strudel warm or cold, dredged with confectioners' sugar and accompanied by the cider sauce.

# tropical fruit salad

| | | **ingredients** |
|---|---|---|
| | very easy | 1 ripe mango |
| | | 1 papaya |
| | serves 4 | 1 small pineapple |
| | | 1¼ cups pineapple |
| | |   or orange juice |
| | 20 minutes + 1 hour to chill | 2 small bananas |
| | — | |

NUTRITIONAL
INFORMATION

| | |
|---|---|
| calories | 154 |
| protein | 2 g |
| carbohydrate | 38 g |
| sugars | 37 g |
| fat | 1 g |
| saturates | 0 g |

Cutting close to the pit, cut a large slice from one side of the mango, then cut another slice from the opposite side. Without breaking the skin, cut the flesh in the segments into squares, then push the skin inside out to expose the cubes, and cut away from the skin. Use a sharp knife to peel the remaining center section and cut the flesh away from the pit into cubes. Reserve any juice and put in a serving bowl with the mango flesh.

Cut the papaya in half and discard the seeds. Remove the skin and cut the flesh into cubes. Peel the pineapple, remove the center core and as many "eyes" as possible, and cut the flesh into chunks. Add both fruits to the mango.

Pour in the fruit juice and chill the mixture in the refrigerator for about 1 hour. Just before serving, slice the bananas and add the slices to the fruit salad.

# apple & honey water ice

| | | ingredients |
|---|---|---|
| very easy | | 4 crisp eating apples |
| | | 2 tbsp lemon juice |
| serves 4 | | scant 1 cup water |
| | | 5 tbsp sugar |
| | | 2 tbsp honey |
| 10 minutes + 5–6 hours to freeze | | apple slices, to decorate |
| 20 minutes | | |

**NUTRITIONAL INFORMATION**

| | |
|---|---|
| calories | 175 |
| protein | 0 g |
| carbohydrate | 46 g |
| sugars | 46 g |
| fat | 0 g |
| saturates | 0 g |

Peel and core the apples and cut them into chunks. Put in a pan with the lemon juice and 1 tablespoon of water and heat gently for about 20 minutes, stirring frequently, until soft.

Meanwhile, put the sugar and the remaining water in a pan and heat gently, stirring, until dissolved. Bring to a boil, then boil for 2 minutes. Remove from the heat.

Push the apple through a strainer into a bowl. Stir in the sugar syrup and honey. Let stand until cold.

When cold, pour the mixture into a freezer container. Freeze, uncovered, for 2 hours until the water ice mixture begins to set. Turn the mixture into a bowl and whisk until smooth. Return to the container and freeze for a further 3–4 hours until firm.

Serve decorated with apple slices.

# raspberry creams

| | | ingredients |
|---|---|---|
| | very easy | 2²/₃ cups raspberries |
| | | ³/₄ cup lowfat cottage cheese |
| | serves 4 | 3 tbsp sugar |
| | | ²/₃ cup lowfat plain yogurt |
| | 10 minutes + 1 hour to chill | confectioners' sugar, to decorate |
| | — | |

**NUTRITIONAL INFORMATION**

| | |
|---|---|
| calories | 142 |
| protein | 9 g |
| carbohydrate | 25 g |
| sugars | 25 g |
| fat | 1 g |
| saturates | 1 g |

Reserving a few whole raspberries to decorate, use the back of a spoon to push the raspberries and cottage cheese through a strainer into a bowl.

Stir the sugar and yogurt into the raspberry mixture and stir to blend, then spoon into individual serving dishes. Chill in the refrigerator for about 1 hour.

Serve chilled, decorated with the reserved raspberries and dusted with sifted confectioners' sugar.

# compôte of dried fruit

| | | ingredients |
|---|---|---|
| extremely easy | | 1 tbsp jasmine tea<br>1 ¼ cups boiling water |
| serves 4 | | ¼ cup dried apricots<br>¼ cup dried apple rings<br>¼ cup prunes |
| 25 minutes + 24 hours to marinate | | 1 ¼ cups fresh orange juice |
| — | | |

**NUTRITIONAL INFORMATION**

| | |
|---|---|
| calories | 103 |
| protein | 2 g |
| carbohydrate | 25 g |
| sugars | 25 g |
| fat | 0 g |
| saturates | 0 g |

Put the tea in a pitcher and pour in the boiling water. Let steep for 20 minutes, then strain.

Put the dried fruits in a serving bowl and pour the jasmine tea and orange juice over them. Cover and marinate in the refrigerator for 24 hours.

Serve the compôte well chilled.

# index